THE IMPACT OF
The Academic Achieve

MW01227459

The Impact Of Slavery

Its Effects On The Academic Achievement Of Black Students Today

DR. PATRICIA McQUEEN

Unless otherwise identified, Scripture quotations are from the King James Version of the Holy Bible.

For additional information, please contact:
prof.mcq15@gmail.com

For information about special discounts for bulk purchases please contact the author, Dr. Patricia McQueen

Printed in the United States of America

LIABILITY DISCLAIMER

The issues in this book may be deemed by some as controversial. However, they are researched based and meant to reveal the truth about the issues of racism in American society as it affects the education Black students. By revealing the truth about how racism really started, we will discover that we have all been victims of its ugly effects. Regardless of anyone's interpretation of the issues in this book, let it be understood that the author advocates understanding, healing, and unity between the races, not hatred and division. The author maintains that she is in no way responsible for the actions of any individuals who may think otherwise.

Also, there are no resale rights or private label rights granted when purchasing this book. In other words, it's for your own personal use only.

Dr. Patricia McQueen

THE IMPACT OF SLAVERY: Its Effects On
The Academic Achievement Of Black Students Today

Dr. PATRICIA McQUEEN

TABLE OF CONTENTS

ACKNOWLEDGMENTS

I would like to thank all the great authors of the many books and articles that I read for their contributions to the issues of racism in American society. It is because of your revelations that I was able to compile the information that I needed to produce this book about the American education system. Also, I would like to thank my brother Vernon Johnson, and my daughter Rhonda Johnson, who recommended several of the books that I used as references for this project. I would like to thank my sister, Angela Byrd, for her valuable input as I was writing this book. Furthermore, thank you James Davis, my cousin, for your awesome illustration on the cover of this book. Last, but certainly not least, I would like to thank Dr. Beverly Crockett, who edited this book, and who also encouraged and advised me along the way to completion.

INTRODUCTION

This book comprises an analytical, literary review of the enslavement of Blacks in America, and its impact on the academic achievement of the Black American student.   I will also inject much of my own experiences as an Black American and as an educator. The need for such a book is apparent since state and national statistics show that there has been a constant and alarming gap in the academic achievement scores of Black students and their Caucasian counterparts.

From this point forward, I will refer to Caucasians as Whites and Black Americans as Blacks. These are well-known terms used in our American society for people of European origin and Negro origin respectively.

A U. S. News and World Report article in 2016 on this subject states:

> *The achievement gap between White students and Black students has barely narrowed over the last 50 years, despite nearly a half century of supposed progress in race relations and an increased emphasis on closing such academic discrepancies between groups of students. That's the finding that a new analysis of a landmark education report calls a "national embarrassment."*

"It's remarkable," says Eric Hanushek, Senior Fellow at the Hoover Institution at Stanford University and Research Associate at the National Bureau of Economic Research, who authored the analysis. "I knew that the gap hadn't been closing too much, but when I actually looked at the data I was myself surprised."

The National Assessment of Educational Progress (NAEP), the largest national representative of continuing assessment of the academic progress of American students stated the following:

The academic achievement of both Black and White public school students, as measured by the NAEP, has improved across time. However, the difference or gap, in the achievement between these two groups of students persists; on average, Black students generally score lower than White students. In 2017, Black students had an average score that was 33 points lower than that for White students. (The Nation's Report Card, 2018).

Although much research has been done regarding the issues of Black student education in America, from my review of the literature, I have found that overall, Black educational achievement remains a topic of much concern.

The intent of this book is to aid education professionals, parents, politicians, and students, in understanding the far-reaching effects of slavery on Black American students.

It is important for educators to know the truth about why the academic gap persists to help dispel many of the misconceptions regarding Black American students. It is also important for politicians to create laws that protect the rights of Black students to receive a quality education. This means creating the means by which all schools in America have the resources they need to provide an equal and much desired quality education. It is of utmost importance for parents to understand the effects of slavery on Black American students, to diligently reject inferior public educational facilities, and instead to seek quality public educational facilities for their children.

This book will bring light to the fact that slavery affected the cultural, economic, political, and social/psychological lives of Black people, thereby inhibiting the academic achievements of Black students.

It is my belief that bringing these revelations to light will foster a greater mutual understanding between these particular races (Blacks and Whites). This treatise only refers to Blacks and Whites because these are the major players in the slavery drama in America. I have discovered that there is so much misunderstanding because slavery, as an institution is very difficult for people to face. It was perpetrated on Blacks and Whites. Blacks, because we were the victims, the slaves; Whites, because they were caught up in a horrible lie – a massive propaganda that compelled them to accept and perpetuate the enslavement of another human being.

The Holy Bible says the truth will make you free. Facing the truth will help Black students understand who they really are, and how they should act, as well as react. Facing the truth will dispel a myriad of myths within our communities, both nationally and internationally. Facing the truth will help educators, parents, students, and more, to move forward in the kind of unity that America needs now, more than ever before.

CHAPTER 1

The Slavery Legacy

Black Americans have made significant gains in social, economic, and educational achievements since the Emancipation Proclamation was passed in 1863. Even the possibility of electing an African American President of the United States became reality in the year 2007.

The enormous contributions to the fabric of American history and culture by brilliant and gifted Black Americans have a significant place in American history. However, this was not always the case. From the early 1600's to 1863, the majority of Blacks in America were slaves. Blacks recognized that they were not going to be given credit for the countless contributions they made to American culture. Many of their inventions were stolen or credited to their slave masters. They were considered chattel, with no rights. Except for the mention of slavery, the lives and contributions of Blacks were largely left out of American History textbooks.

The following is a statement regarding Carter G. Woodson's founding of Black History Week in 1926, citing the need for Black American representation in American History textbooks.

> *Disturbed that history textbooks largely ignored America's Black population, Woodson took on the*

challenge of writing Black Americans into the nation's history in "Extra! History of Black." To do this, Woodson established The Association for the Study of Negro Life and History. He also founded the group's widely respected publication, The Journal of Negro History. In 1926, he developed Negro History Week. Woodson believed that the "achievements of the Negro properly set forth will crown him as a factor in early human progress and a maker of modern civilization."

In 1976, the celebration was expanded into Black History Month. However, even as late as 1988, 125 years after slavery was abolished, History textbooks were still deficient in promoting the contributions of Blacks. It is because of Black History Month that the names of great Black American scholars, doctors, lawyers, politicians, teachers, clergy, entrepreneurs, builders, inventors, writers, poets, and artists of every genre have emerged. Many lives were sacrificed, many dreams were shattered, many hopes were dashed, but the steadfast conviction of Blacks who believe that their lives do matter prevailed, and continues to prevail.

However, this is largely a Black celebration, but in mainstream America, namely White America, the legacy that has been emphasized and passed on to future generations of Black Americans and the world, is a legacy of slavery, the dark side of our past.

The side that shows our greatness, our value, and our worth has been grossly ignored. Furthermore, when a Black person is finally recognized for some great achievement, you hear the phrase "he was the first Black or she was the first Black to ...." It is not because the achievement itself is innately uncommon among Black people, it is because the opportunities for such achievements are so rare. Opportunities have been prevented or disallowed because of stigma; the negative social identity, which was born out of slavery and upheld in the education arena. This stigma has spawned racism.

Perhaps there are a privileged few who, because of fortunate circumstances, have escaped the boundaries of hatred and bigotry associated with being an offspring of Black slaves; nevertheless, it is the masses of Black Americans who are impacted (whether knowingly or unknowingly) by the legacy of slavery.

Though some Americans don't believe it, some don't even understand it, it would be difficult to deny that the stigma of slavery still plagues Black Americans even into the 21st century.

THE IMPACT OF SLAVERY: Its Effects On
The Academic Achievement of Black Students Today

CHAPTER 2

Racism

The dictionary defines racism as, *"the belief that some races are inherently superior (physically, intellectually, or culturally) to others, and therefore have a right to dominate them. In the United States, racism, particularly by whites against blacks, has created profound racial tension and conflict in virtually all aspects of American society."*

Racism is so ingrained in the American psyche, that in many cases the first thing a person sees when he/she meets another person is the color of their skin; or when referring to someone in a conversation, the question inevitably arises, "Was he/she Black, or was he/she White?" It is a social construct that has been so insidious that it is hardly recognized for what it is in many social, behavioral, and psychological contexts. It may appear to be harmless; nevertheless, it continues to create division among people because of the color of their skin, and is therefore self-perpetuating. I like the way Wachtel said it: *"Racism promotes enduring patterns of inequality...the roots of racism lie in our nation's tragic and appalling history and in our failure fully to transcend it."*

Young Black people today can see the bigotry and hatred that existed by merely looking at how their ancestors were represented in American history, but that bigotry and hatred have been largely covert in our contemporary society so that young Blacks don't recognize it. Nevertheless, now bigotry and hatred are beginning to boldly rear their ugly heads again, through all the recent issues concerning racial discrimination. There is much concern now for the many incidences of police shooting Blacks for unjustifiable and superfluous reasons, and many protest groups are arising because of this.

Even in 2016, during the presidential campaign, the issue of race is brought to the forefront of American politics. Some prominent politicians have shamelessly used race as a platform to engender fear and mistrust among the people.

Furthermore, the Ku Klux Klan and other White supremacy groups are emerging and trying to gain a foothold in our political arena. It is apparent that racism is alive and living large in America.

As of this writing, our own President, Barack Obama, who is African American, has had to endure racial slurs and degrading images of himself throughout his career. Phrases like "taking the government back," and "let's make America great again," have all emerged during his presidency, as though America has somehow declined since he took office. The fact is, however, when Obama took office, he inherited a huge financial recession from the previous administration. It was the Obama administration that brought the American economy back from the brink of disaster, created millions of new jobs, and started the country moving again.

As an Black American, growing up in the 1950's and 60's in America, I was insulated against much of the overt racism, because I grew up in the District of Columbia (D.C.). In those days, D.C. was predominantly Black in the area where I lived. There were Whites on the west side, and on Capitol Hill, but the city itself was referred to as the "Chocolate City," because of its large Black population. I went to all Black schools until my junior year in high school. However, television, movies, magazines, and textbooks had little or no Black representation. As I recall, the only Black people on television were those that played maids, butlers, or slaves; and they had to portray a shuffling, degrading demeanor. Even the people on the continent of Africa were depicted as savages and cannibals. These were all stereotypes that were used to maintain the idea that Whites were better than Blacks.

We did have the Ebony and Jet magazines that were popular among Black people, and were all about us. The textbooks, however, only represented Blacks as slaves.

As kids, we didn't have a complete understanding of what it meant to be Black, but we knew that there was something wrong with it. We knew that there were places we couldn't go, and things we couldn't do because of it.

We were trying to be white back then. We wanted straight, or "good" hair, thin lips, narrow noses, and to talk "proper." If your hair was kinky, your lips were thick, or your skin was dark, you were made to feel less than others. Having light skin meant that you were somehow better than your other Black brothers and sisters.

Even among family members, there was jealousy or mistreatment because of light-skin vs. dark-skin. I remember, as a light skinned girl growing up, I was referred to by some family members as "that ole' yellow gal."

White people also promoted this idea. The lighter your skin, the easier they accepted you. Even today, in the 21st century, I've heard so-called dark-skinned people say that they don' like the color of their skin. I've heard someone say that another person was blessed because they had light skin. Let me reiterate; the effects of slavery are far-reaching.

As Black people, we have had to go through so many unnecessary, or perhaps they were necessary, changes to reinforce our upward mobility in American society. We have had to define ourselves many times. During Slavery, besides being called many denigrating names such as niggers, nigras, coons, and darkies, we were referred to as Blacks or Negroes, which literally means black in Spanish and Portuguese, and refers to Black Africans. Negro was considered the correct term for Black Americans from the 18th century to the mid-20th century. There was a time, as I was growing up, that calling someone "black" was an insult. You could get killed for calling someone black. It was a demeaning term. Then, there was a time when we referred to ourselves a colored. This appeared to be acceptable.

Eventually, during the Civil Rights era, in the late 1960's, the term Black was again accepted as James Brown shouted, "Say it loud, I'm Black and I'm proud!" We no longer wanted to be White, as we started sporting our Afros and Dashikis. I even started smearing on coco butter in the sun to darken my skin. How crazy was that! It was a proud time to be Black.

During that same era, other songs by James Brown such as, "I Don't Want Nobody to Give Me Nothing, (Open Up the Door, I'll Get it Myself)," inspired us to want to move out of the ghettos. It helped us to realize that we could make it and be somebody.

Finally, we adopted the term "African American," which was first used by African immigrants who were naturalized citizens of the United States, not descendants of slaves. However, in 1988, Jesse Jackson at a news conference, encouraged all of us to use the term African American when referring to Blacks.

From 1954 to 1968, the Civil Rights Movement brought about a pivotal change in the lives of Black Americans. It was a tumultuous and violent time between Blacks and Whites. During this time, many laws were changed, which brought an end to many forms of de jure segregation

(segregation that is imposed by law) in all sectors of our society, especially public schools.

Although the laws prohibited segregation, de facto segregation, racial discrimination, and many forms of repression continued to be the norm. As Martin Luther King, Jr. so aptly stated: "You can't legislate morals. The job must be done through education and religion."

When I graduated from high school, began to mature, go out into the world to make my own way, I began to understand discrimination and prejudice. One of the first jobs I got before going to college was that of a teacher's aide. Part of my job was to chaperone the students to a white school on the west side of D.C.

The first thing the White teacher asked me was, "Do you think they can learn?" I was shocked, and I didn't know what to say, at first. Then I said, "Of course they can learn." I wondered how she could ask me such a ridiculous question. Of course, this was the prevailing attitude of White teachers.

This was an example of the gross misunderstanding and erroneous belief that pervaded the White community regarding Black people. Where did these erroneous beliefs originate? Read on, and you will understand how this belief developed – The Indoctrination of Whites and Blacks.

CHAPTER 3

The Indoctrination of Whites and Blacks

The enslavement of Blacks in 17th Century America has left a legacy of institutionalized racism that is still inveterately rooted in American society more than 300 years later. From its inception, this enslavement was propagated for both economic and political exploitation by the White founding fathers.

An ideology had to be developed which could justify using Black people as slaves – which could also compel the average White person to accept the enslavement of another person. That ideology was racism. Lerone Bennett stated:

> ...*racism, is not an individual idea or peculiarity, but an institutionalized ideology that commits the institutions of a society to the destruction of a people because of race. The idea developed by the Virginians (and Americans) was simple and profitable. The idea was that all Whites were biologically superior to all Blacks, who were infidels and heathens; a dangerous and accursed people who embodied an evil principle that made them dangerous to the morals and the politics of the community. The truth or falsity of this idea disturbed few men then (or now). The only thing that mattered was that this idea or something like it was necessary to*

*justify past, present, and future aggression
against Blacks.*

From this ideology of racism, the colonial aristocracy developed a system of domination of Blacks that permeated every aspect of life. A careful and deliberate propaganda campaign was promulgated to solicit the support of every White person and White institution, both social and governmental – a campaign of separation and subordination. The basis for their campaign was to portray Blacks as something less than human.

A calculated division between Whites and Blacks had to be created if this system of slavery were to survive. Blacks and Whites had to be taught the meaning of Blackness and Whiteness in such a way as to create the division, and this division was preserved by force and violence, and sanctioned by laws.

In the ensuing pages, we will look at the provenance of slavery – ot how it all began. It was the basis upon which every political, social economic, moral, and psychological decision was made in the beginning and may very well be today. Black vs. White has been the weltanschauung (one's world view or conception of life) of American society.

The following excerpt from a letter written by a man named Willie Lynch, whose name became eponymous with lynching, is an example of the many forms of systematic indoctrination that was perpetrated upon Blacks and Whites to promote division between the two races. In 1712, Willie Lynch wrote the following:

> I have a foolproof method for controlling your Black slaves. I guarantee every one of you that if installed correctly it will control the slaves for at least 300 years. My method is simple. Any member of your family or your overseer can use it. I have outlined a number of differences among the slaves, and I take these differences and make them bigger. I use fear, distrust, and envy for control purposes.... Take this simple little list of differences and think about them. On top of my list is "age," but it's there only because it starts with an "A." The second is "COLOR" or shade; there is intelligence, size, sex, size of plantations and status on plantations, attitude of owners, whether the slaves live in the valley, on a hill, East, West, North, South, have fine hair, course hair, or is tall or short. Now that you have a list of differences, I shall give you an outline of action, but before that, I shall assure you that distrust is stronger than trust and envy stronger than adulation, respect or admiration. Don't forget you must pitch the old Black male vs. the young Black male, and the young Black male against the old Black male. You must use the dark skin slaves vs. the light skin slaves, and the light skin slaves vs. the dark skin

slaves. You must use the female vs. the male; and the male vs. the female. You must also have your White servants and overseers distrust all Blacks. It is necessary that your slaves trust and depend on us. They must love, respect, and trust only us. Gentlemen, these kits are your keys to control. Use them. If used intensely for one year, the slaves themselves will remain perpetually distrustful of each other. Have your wives and children use them; never miss an opportunity.....

The Black slaves, after receiving this indoctrination, shall carry on and will become self-refueling and self-generating for hundreds of years, maybe thousands...

This is just an excerpt from the letter on how to control Blacks in order to maintain slavery; there is much more. It was clear from this letter that Willie Lynch was indoctrinating Caucasians to mistrust, fear, and misuse Black people. It has been 155 years since the Emancipation Proclamation, and Black Americans are still enduring the effects of those racists' tactics.

The institution of slavery promoted racism, and left a stigma that Blacks have had to endure unto this day. It is that negative social identity that is the premise for understanding how Slavery impacted the academic achievement of Black students today.

I considered three areas for discussion that emerged from the literature review as being paramount in understanding how the institution of slavery is connected to the academic achievement of our Black youth. First, it is important to understand the slaves – their experiences, their attitudes, their feelings – to dispel this notion that Blacks were less than human and therefore, fit for slavery. It is also important to understand that because of the slavery experience, Blacks were affected socially and psychologically, and this has been passed on from generation to generation.

Thus, I have included the, "The Life of the American Slave." This is a collection of testimonies from slaves and ex-slaves which reveals the almost ineffable anguish that was felt during their life of slavery. (Blassingame, 1977; Starobin, 1974; Douglas, 2003; Clinton, 2004; Davis and Gates, 1985 Woodson, 1969) It also reveals the fact that, though the slaves were denied formal education, it was their common sense and good judgment that sustained them and allowed them to take care of the slaveholders and their families.

Secondly, it was of major importance to emphasize the role of the government in the perpetuation of this "master/slave" mentality, and in sanctioning the division of the races. In the beginning, the government established laws to control the slaves and protect the slave-owners. After the Civil War and the abolition of Slavery, southern states began a system of segregation and subordination of Blacks through the creation of new laws in their state constitutions. (Davis, 2008) These new laws were designed to segregate the races in public places; especially schools, and to prevent Black men from voting. Several laws and ordinances have been included in this writing to show how they were inextricably connected to the relationship between slave and master, and how they consistently relegated free Blacks to a subordinate role in American society. This section is entitled, "The Role that Government Played."

The final section is "The Social Stigma Legacy." In this section, you will see the role that stigma has played in our schools, how our black youth have responded, and what can be done, so our Black youth have a better chance at success in the educational arena. Let's look back to where racism started.

CHAPTER 4

The Life of the American Slave

There are many accounts of how the slave-owners and proponents of slavery justified the establishment of such a heinous institution. There are also many accounts from abolitionists and opponents of slavery who promoted their views. However, after an extensive review of a mountain of literature from various noted authors, I immediately recognized the exigency of reporting the slaves' experiences from their own minds. Marcus Garvey wrote:

"It takes the slaves to interpret the feeling of the slave; it takes the unfortunate man to interpret the spirit of his unfortunate brother; and so it takes the suffering Negro to interpret the spirit of his comrade."

The following is an excerpt from *Freedom's Journal*:

"We wish to plead our case. Too long have others spoken for us. Too long has the publick been deceived by misrepresentations, in things which concern us dearly [italics added].

Freedom's Journal was the first Black American newspaper founded in 1827, by John B. Russwurm and Samuel E. Cornish in New York City, in response to the negative portrayals of Black people in White-owned newspapers. It was also a forum for the discouragement of the re-enslavement of free Black Americans, because many of the White editors were advocating re-enslavement of New York's free Black Americans. This journal was a very significant Black voice that bellowed out that Blacks are not to be equated with the beast of the field. Black people are rational human beings who "are able to see the truth through the veil of other [people's] mystifying and reality negating revelations; who insist upon seeing and portraying ourselves through the revelation of our own experiences and interpretations." (Walker, 2001, p.24)

I can relate to the negative portrayals of Blacks because of my experiences in the late 60's and 70's. Black people in American have always been characterized by some stereotype that does not portray a true image of who we are. Yes, we wore afros and dashikis, and these were meant to show a people proud of their heritage, and to foster a sense of relief of the burden of wondering whether we were "white" enough.

Yes, we loved our music, we loved to dance, and we loved sports; and we excelled greatly in these areas, but these were not the only things we did well. When given the opportunity, we were and are able to do anything we set our minds to. Regardless of how we reacted to certain situations, our images were always presented as some extreme caricature devoid of dignity and/or intelligence. Even the roles we were given in the movies or on television were extremely comical, and might have been acceptable if there had been other roles that portrayed us as responsible, serious-minded individuals, who contributed something meaningful and worthwhile to our society.

Not only that, we had to work harder than anyone else in order to get any kind of credit for what we did. At the same time, because of the imperialistic attitude on the part of many Whites, the best Black American achievement is still second best to the most menial achievement of a White person.

I have seen credit given to many Whites when they truly did not deserve it, and Blacks who excelled, even far beyond their White counterparts in that same area, denied the credit because of the color of their skin.

As a matter of fact, I knew a young man who was a very poor student in my class. I counseled him on the importance of learning how to read well, so that he would be able get a good job. He told me it didn't matter; he would get a job anyway because he was White. This is the result of that indoctrination I mentioned earlier in this writing.

However, we have come a long way since those days, and we do have more significant roles and are portrayed in a much better light in society, but the stereotypes and racist attitudes still persist in many people's minds.

Be that as it may, let's further discuss the life of the American slave. From newspapers or letters written by slaves themselves, and personal accounts of notable slaves such as Harriett Tubman and Frederick Douglass, the mind of Blacks was revealed. These revelations did not come from so called barbarous, savage creatures, but from human beings suffering from the degradation and anguish of enslavement. It was through those 18th and 19th century texts that Black men and women refuted the bogus assertion that they were less than human.

According to Davis and Gates, The Black American slave narratives form a large body of literature, but have been largely ignored by historians. In 1926, it was Carter G. Woodson who first published seven letters written by slaves in his work, *"The Mind of the Negro as Reflected in Letters Written During the Crisis, 1800-1860."*

Robert Starobin also included 48 letters written by slaves in his book written in 1974, "Blacks in Bondage: Letters of American Slaves." This is a collection of letters written by slaves who recorded explicit feelings about being Black and being in bondage. The words recorded there express complexity and diversity of thought and feeling about slavery and being Black, and offer glimpses into the interior lives of a number of American slaves.

In addition, John W. Blassingame compiled yet another huge volume of slave narratives in his book, *"Slave Testimony: Two Centuries of Letters, Speeches, Interviews, and Autobiographies,"* in 1977.

Davis and Gates presented a collection of essays and reviews of the slave narratives in their book, *"The Slave's Narratives."* This was a compilation of critical reviews of slave narratives, initially written for historians, critics, economists, folklorists, anthropologists, sociologists, and literary critics, to facilitate their understanding of the importance these narratives hold in historiography, and to encourage literary critics to also study their form and structure as an important literary genre.

Blassingame's volume, *"Slave Testimony,"* contains many of the same narratives that were compiled by the aforementioned authors, therefore his volume was used to extract the many examples that are included herein.

I have also included the testimony of Harriet Tubman and Frederick Douglass, notable ex-slaves whose testimonies are well documented. Their experiences as slaves corroborate the other testimonies compiled by Blassingame.

Although we must assume that no written text is a completely thorough picture of the slaves' lives, regardless of who writes it, Blassingame and other historians who have contributed to the compilation of these narratives have been careful to select a group of slave narratives that have been deemed authentic. Some of these testimonies were written by the slaves themselves, and others were written or edited for the slaves, by men who were noted for their integrity.

According to Blassingame, these editors, for whom biographical data is available, were professional people who were experienced in the separation of truth and fiction, and who knew how to apply rules of evidence to accurately portray men and events.

Most of these editors were not connected to the abolitionists' movement; however, some were members of the American Freedmen's Inquiry Commission who were appointed to gather information for the Commission. This will be discussed in more detail later in this writing. Many of their interests were sparked by sensational trials of fugitive slaves; some were motivated by their interest in history; still others were pastors and ministers who advocated toleration of slavery, because they would not have been able to preach otherwise.

An example of a noted editor is Samuel A. Eliot, a graduate of Harvard College and the Harvard Divinity School. He served in the Massachusetts General Court, as the Mayor of Boston, Treasurer of Harvard, Congressman, and as a contributor to the *North American Review* and the *Christian Examiner*. Another editor, David Wilson, was a New York Lawyer, state legislator, poet and school superintendent. Yet another example was William G. Eliot, a a graduate of Columbia University and the Harvard Divinity School. He was a reformer, philanthropist, pastor and founder of Washington University at St. Louis, who advocated gradual emancipation. Last, but certainly not least, Charles Campbell, a descendant of Governor Alexander Spotswood, a graduate of the College of New Jersey, was the editor of the *American Statesman* in Petersburg, frequent contributor to the *Virginia Historical Register, the Southern Literary Messenger,* and the *Farmer's Register.* He was also an avid collector of old manuscripts, and was noted for his remarkable research and accuracy. These were only a few of the noteworthy editors of this compilation of slave testimonies. There were many more.

The narratives took several forms: letters: 1736-1864; speeches: 1837-1862; newspaper and magazine interviews: 1827-1863; American Freedmen's Inquiry Commission Interviews: 1863; interviews by scholars: 1872-1938; and autobiographies published in periodicals and books: 1828-1878.

Though the narratives cover a broad spectrum of slavery life, the examples I chose to include in this writing were meant to convey the sufferings of the slaves, the intelligence with which they dealt with their plight, and the fact that freedom was always uppermost in their minds. These accounts of the slavery experience are gruesome to say the least, and unbelievable. When I shared these accounts with others, some displayed an attitude of incredulity. My experience was corroborated by William Lloyd Garrison, a prominent American abolitionist, journalist, and social reformer. He wrote in the preface of the "Narrative of the Life of Frederick Douglass"

> *"So profoundly ignorant of the nature of slavery are many persons, that they are stubbornly incredulous, whenever they read or listen to any recital of the cruelties which are daily inflicted on its victims. They do not deny that the slaves are held as property, but that terrible fact seems to convey to their minds no idea of injustice, exposure to outrage, or savage barbarity. Tell them of cruel scourgings, of mutilations and brandings, of scenes of pollution and blood... they affect to be greatly indignant at such enormous exaggerations, such wholesale misstatements, such abominable libels on the character of the Southern planters...Skeptics of this character abound in society."*

These slave experiences were real - the effects of which reached through time and space to a people of the 21st century who are still susceptible to their persistent sting. Let me note here that these , testimonies may not contain the standard English spelling, grammar, and punctuation acceptable in 21st century America, however, they are quite legible, comprehensible, and full of wisdom and intellect. Also, for those who are not aware, during that era and for many years after, Blacks in America were referred to as Negroes.

The following are excerpts from each of these forms of testimonies:

Letters Written by the Slaves Themselves

Henry Bibb, born in 1815, escaped from his master at about the age of twenty-seven. Before that time he had witnessed murder, incest, and adultery. Bibb fled to Detroit, where he was trying to raise enough money to buy the freedom of his wife and child, but before he could do this, his wife was sold off as a mistress to another slave owner. Bibb subsequently devoted his life to the abolition of slavery. He abhorred slavery and became the quintessential author and lecturer on Black slavery during his time, having experienced its horrors first hand. These are excerpts from two of several letters he wrote to his master in 1852:

> *While on the other hand, your church sanctions the buying and selling of men, women, and children: robbing men of their wives, and parents of their offspring – the violation of the whole of the Decalogue, by permitting the profanation of the Sabbath; committing of theft, murder, incest, and adultery, which is constantly done by church members holding slaves and form the very essence of slavery.*
>
> *I have oft heard you say that a slave who is well fed, and clothed, was far better off than a "free Negro,"*

who had no master to provide for and take care of him. Now with all candour, in answer to this proslavery logic, let me ask who is it that takes care of the slave holders and their families? Who is it that clears up the forests, cultivates the land, manages the stock, husbands to grain and prepares it for the table? Who is it that digs from the cotton, sugar, and rice fields the means with which to build southern cities, steam boats, school houses and churches? I answer that it is the slaves that perform this labor, and yet they or their children are not permitted to enjoy any of the benefits of these institutions..... Oh! tell me not then sir, that a man is happier and better off in a state of chattel bondage than in a state of freedom. Freedom to act for oneself though poorly clad and fed with a dry crust is glorious when coparedd with American Slavery.

George Moses Horton, a slave who learned to read and write on his own, with no formal schooling, was a lover of poetry. He wrote a letter to Mr. William Lloyd Garrison, editor of a Boston paper, in the hopes of publishing some of his poetry. The following is an excerpt of the letter and a few lines from his poem entitled, "The Poets Feeble Petition."

Letter: Sir, ...I am necessarily constrained, to apply to your honor for assistance in carrying my original work into publick execution, while I gratify your curiosity in resolving the problem whether a Negro has any genious or not. Sir I am not alone actuated by pecuniary motive, but upon the whole, to spread the blaze of African genious and thus dispel the sceptic gloom so prevalent in many parts of the country.

Poem: Bewailing mid the ruthless wave, I lift my feeble hand to thee. Let me no longer be a slave, but drop these fetters and be free.

Speeches

Listed below is an excerpt from a speech by a slave named Johnson, who was introduced by a member of the Massachusetts Anti-Slavery Society in Boston. Evidently Johnson had become a free man, as mandated by his owner before his death. He was not a professional speaker like some of the freed abolitionists slaves had become. His testimony was considered more personal and specific by Blassingame, because of this fact:

One day my master was dining with a gentleman who had a wife as Black as dat hat. A young colored woman, as likely for her color as any lady in dis assembly (a laugh) waited on table. She happened to spill a little gravy on the gown of her mistress. The gentleman took his carving knife, dragged her out to the wood pile, and cut her head off; den wash his hands, come in and fiinsh his dinner like nothing had happened.

This same man, Johnson, reported several gruesome experiences like this one. Among them were seeing slaves whipped and brine thrown on the wounds; slaves being beaten and left all night in the cold to freeze to death; slaves being whipped for trying to worship.

Newspapers and Magazines: 1827-1863

This article was written by Isaac T. Hopper, for the National Anti-Slavery Standard, September 9, 1841. Mr. Hopper interviewed a woman named Ann Garrison. After years of slavery, Mrs. Garrison was finally manumitted by a man named John H. Hicks who paid two hundred-fifty dollars for her freedom. She was filled with joy, until she realized that she had to leave her three children, who would probably be sold as slaves, never to be seen by their mother again. She said, "I was filled with the utmost anguish. Parting with them seemed more than I could bear." This sort of testimony was prevalent throughout the narratives, and appeared to provoke more anguish among the slaves than any other.

Another article, written for the Anti-Slavery Reporter, 1841, was similar. In his interview, Madison Jefferson stated that one of his sisters had been sold, and many tears were shed by the whole family, but that they had to hide their grief for fear of reprisal – "they would give them something to cry for." He reported that they always dreaded being separated. "We have a dread constantly on our minds, for we don't know how long master may keep us, nor into whose hands we may fall."

American Freedmen's Inquiry Commission Interviews 1863

The American Freedmen's Inquiry Commission (AFIC) was an organization established by Edwin McMasters Stanton, the U. S. Secretary of War, in 1863, to investigate the status of the slaves and freed slaves after the Civil War. The AFIC commissioners, James McKaye, Robert Dale Owens, and Samuel Gridley however, were advocates of emancipation, and had gained the confidence of the slaves who were anxious to "talk to them in order to prove that they were ready for freedom and willing to fight to obtain it."

The secretaries of the commission, J.M. Yerrington and George T. Chapman, recorded practically all the accounts word for word. Some of the questions the interviewers would ask the slaves are as follows:

- How did your master treat you?
- Have you seen any forms of cruel punishment?
- Did slaves want to be free?
- Are slaves willing to enlist in the army?
- What is the present condition of Blacks in the area?

It was the answers to these questions and many more, that helped form the framework for Reconstruction, 1866-1877, which was the process of readmitting the southern states to the Union after the Civil War.

The following are examples of some of the cruelest experiences related by the slaves in these interviews: After making a woman stretch out her stomach, tying her to a stake, and whipping her mercilessly, the master kicked her in the mouth for crying, and finally poured hot wax on her wounds. Her only crime was burning the edges of waffles. A hole was made in the ground for a pregnant woman's stomach while she lay on the ground to be beaten. Several slaves were stacked vertically on top of one another in stocks, and given a strong laxative which made them drop feces on one another. Most pregnant women had to work just as hard as anyone else from sun-up to sun-down, unless the master's wife made an appeal to her husband to lighten their loads. There were many more examples, equally as cruel or even more so, but too many to mention here.

The interviews also revealed that men and women yearned for freedom, and some were able to save up enough money to buy it – even if it took a life time. One man reported that he saved fifty dollars a year for twenty years to buy his freedom. He was hired out buy his master, as many slaves were, and though he had to give the master most of his money, he was able to put away a few pennies at a time for himself to buy his freedom.

Regarding questions about self-reliance after the Civil war, several responses were noted to say that the government should help Blacks for a while, and protect them until they were able to be self-supporting. They did not trust the White man. They thought he would take their land or cheat them in some way. However, they wanted to eventually be self- supporting. Most of the slaves – men and women – had excellent skills that would prepare them for a life outside of slavery. Many of them were hired out by their masters for various occupations. There were construction workers, Blacksmiths, riggers, stevedores, waiters, clerks, mechanics, factory workers, railroad workers, domestics and many other occupations.

It was the finding of the Commission that the Black race "lacked no essential aptitude for civilization;" that the Negro was a hard worker, exhibited self-respect and pride in his work; that once freed, he would become a useful member of society.

The Testimony of Frederick Douglass

Frederick Douglass was born Frederick Augustus Washington Bailey, in 1818, on a plantation in Talbot County, Maryland. After his escape to the North, he changed his name to Frederick Douglass. Through the ravages of slavery, he managed to educate himself, and he was determined to become a free man. The testimony of his life as a slave corroborates the cruelty and brutality of the slave owner. He eventually became a powerful orator, writer, newspaper editor, and eloquent spokesperson for the freedom of Black Americans. His work still has an amazing influence on civil rights advocates today. He wrote:

> *To make a contented slave, you must make a thoughtless one. It is necessary to darken his moral and mental vision, and as far as possible, to annihilate his power of reason. He must be able to detect no inconsistencies in slavery. The man that takes his earnings must be able to convince him that he has a perfect right to do so. It must not depend upon mere force; the slave must know no Higher Law than his master's will. The whole relationship must not only demonstrate, to his mind, its necessity, but its absolute rightfulness. If there be one crevice through which a single drop can fall, it will certainly rust off the slave's chain.*

This statement corroborates certain passages of the Willie Lynch letter which urge the slave owners to..

> *break them from one form of mental life to another.. do a complete reversal of the mind... in other words break the will to resist. Take the meanest and most restless nigger, strip him of his clothes in front of the*

remaining male niggers, the female and the nigger infant; tar and feather him, tie each leg to a different horse faced in opposite directions, set him afire and beat both horses to pull him apart in front of the remaining niggers.

Lynch goes on the say that you must break the female by beating her within an inch of her life. Reverse her role of being psychologically dependent on the male nigger by destroying his image. This will cause her to move into a "frozen independent state," and she will raise her offspring to take these reversal roles. Fearing the young male's life, she will psychologically train him to be mentally weak and dependent but physically strong.

This was Willie Lynch's plan for keeping the slaves from rising up in rebellion, and for keeping the slave economy sound.

The Testimony of Harriet Tubman

Harriet Tubman was called the Moses of her people. She led hundreds of slaves to their freedom on what was eventually known as the "Underground Railroad." Not only did she lead slaves to freedom, but she worked as a nurse and caretaker for wounded Blacks in the Civil War. In addition, Ms. Tubman was a scout and spy for the Union Army, and she was the only woman who officially led men into battle during the Civil War. She became a much sought after speaker on the abolitionist circuit.

As a slave, she suffered many acts of cruelty just as other slaves. During her younger years, when Harriet was trying to prevent the beating of a slave, she was struck in the head by a lead weight which was meant for the man she was defending. She said, "It broke my skull and cut a piece of that shawl clean off and drove it into my head. They carried me to the house all bleeding and fainting. I had no bed, no place to lie down on at all, and they lay me on the seat of the loom, and I stayed there all that day and the next."

She was so gravely ill that she was not expected to survive. As a result of this blow to the head, Harriet would occasionally fall into a deep lethargic sleep from which it was almost impossible to awaken her. These sleeping spells would come on her without warning, even while she was on the Underground Railroad trail. She would suffer this malady for the rest of her life.

These testimonies are just a glimpse into the life of the Black American slave. However, this brief account is enough for one to understand and recognize the soul of a people who were in fact strong "people," not something less than human, and who were determined to survive with the hope of someday being free.

It took hard work and the sacrifice of many lives to become free. It took the help of Blacks and Whites, who were appalled at this abomination which was perpetrated upon American society, to break this system of slavery.

It took the changing and repeal of many laws – laws which were created and protected by the American Constitution. The following section reveals how slavery was deeply embedded in the political and legal structure of the nation.

THE IMPACT OF SLAVERY: Its Effects On
The Academic Achievement of Black Students Today

CHAPTER 5

The Role That Government Played

Frederick Douglass wrote in his own words:

These shameful laws, are not the natural expression of the moral sentiment of Ohio, but the servile work of pandering politicians who, to conciliate the favor of slaveholders and win their way into political power, have enacted these infernal laws.

Frederick Douglass was on a speaking tour in Ohio when he wrote these words in a letter to the *National Anti-Slavery Standard*, a newspaper published by William Lloyd Garrison. He had experienced many acts of prejudice while touring. He said, "Ohio laws prohibited Blacks from testifying against Whites, thus giving them a 'Thug' mentality and permitting them to insult, cheat, and plunder Blacks with the utmost impunity."

These slave codes to which Douglass was referring had been in existence since the inception of slavery in America. The earliest known arrival of Blacks was in 1619, in Jamestown, VA. During that time, statutes were imposed on a case by case basis, by judges who were trying to please the White power structure.

It was the Virginia colonists that led the way for the institutionalization of slavery. Other colonists followed Virginia's leadership in developing slavery laws. Around

1659, Virginia made a direct reference to Blacks as slaves when it passed Act XVI, which reduced the import duties for the Dutch and other foreigners bringing in slaves. This was a financial incentive to promote the value of slave labor, to encourage the trafficking of slaves, and it was accomplished by legislation.

Thus, the campaign to promote racism emerged. Slave laws had to be enacted, if slavery and racism were going to prevail.   The following are examples of laws enacted to control Blacks and to protect the slave-owners. Though the name of certain states are mentioned here, these laws were prevalent throughout the slave states.

> *Louisiana – "A slave is one who is in the power of a master to whom he belongs. The master may sell him, dispose of his person, his industry and his labor. He can do nothing, possess nothing, nor acquire anything, but what must belong to his master." (Civil Code, Art. 35)*

> *"Slaves shall always be reputed and considered real estate; shall, as such, be subject to be mortgaged, according to the rules prescribed by law, and they shall be seized and sold as real estate."* Statute of June 1806

Such was the definition of a slave in each of the slave states – some laws included words such a *chattel personal* and *personal property*. "This maxim of the civil law, the genuine and degrading principle of slavery, inasmuch as it places the slave upon a level with *brute* animals, prevails universally in the slaveholding states."

Wheeler's Law of Slavery, was a regular law book, made for the use of slaveholders. It was a compilation of all U. S. and state court decisions made on the subject of slavery. The following are several decisions by the courts taken from this book:

> *"They are, however, liable, as chattels, to be sold by the master at his pleasure, and may be taken in execution of payment of his debts."*

> *"Slaves, from their nature, are CHATTELS, and were put in the hands of executors, before the act of 1792."*

> *"In Maryland, the issue," (i.e., of female slaves) "is considered not an accessory, but as a part of the use, like that of other female animals."* (1 Har. & McHen. Rep., 160, 352; 1 Har. & John's Rep., 526; 1 Hayw. Rep., 335)

> *Suppose a brood mare be hired for five years, the foals belong to him who has a part of the use of the dam. (2 Black. Com., 290; 1 Hayw. Rep., 335.) The slave, in Maryland, in this respect, is placed on no higher or different ground."*

> *"Slaves may be sold and transferred from one to another without any statutory restriction or limitation, as to the separation of parents and children."*

"Slaves have no legal right in things, real or personal; but whatever they may acquire, belongs in point of law, to their masters. Slaves can make no contract."

"A slave cannot even contract matrimony, the association which takes place among slaves, and is called marriage, being properly designated by the word contubernium, a relation which has no sanctity."

"The master may wholly forbid and prevent the education, the moral, and religious instruction of his slaves."

"Any person may inflict twenty lashes on the bare back of a slave found without license on the plantation or without the limits of the town to which he belongs."

"If any slave shall presume to strike any White person, such slave, upon trial and conviction before the justice or justices, according to the directions of this act, shall for the first offense, suffer such punishment as the said justice or justices shall, in his or their discretion, think fit, not extending to life or limb; and for the second offense, suffer DEATH."

".. to teach a slave to read or write, or sell or give him any book, (Bible, not excepted) or pamphlet, is punished with 39 lashes, or imprisonment, if the offender be a free Negro; but if a White, then a fine of $200. ... teaching slaves to read and write tends to dissatisfaction in their minds, and to produce rebellion."

I would be remiss if I did not mention the Fugitive Slave Law. There were several that were passed. These laws were a direct result of politicians exploiting Black Americans for wealth and political expediency. One such law was enacted to settle the differences between the North and the South in an attempt to keep the Union together. This law was a part of the Compromise of 1850. During this time, the United States was expanding and adding states and territories. In order to appease slave-state politicians, who wanted to maintain a balance between slave states and free states, the Fugitive Slave Law was passed. It required citizens to assist in the recovery of fugitive slaves. It also denied a fugitive's right to a jury trial.

These are examples of the many laws enacted to preserve slavery before the emancipation of Blacks. America had created a slave society – the complete antithesis of the principles upon which it was founded.

After the Civil War, there was a period called Reconstruction. This was a time when the Union was attempting to correct the injustices of slavery, and to repair the breach in the Union. It was an effort by Whites and Blacks to redefine the responsibilities of government. It was an exciting time for freedmen. With the passage of the 13th, 14th, and 15th Amendments to the Constitution, and the Civil Rights Act of 1866, Black Americans were allowed to vote, participate in the political process, purchase land, seek employment and use public facilities. However, these rights were short-lived.

President Andrew Johnson, who succeeded Abraham Lincoln, allowed the states that had seceded to rejoin the Union as long as they abrogated slavery, paid their war debt, and pledged loyalty to the Union. However, Johnson was a firm believer in states' rights and basically left it up to the states to govern their own affairs.

Southern states began enacting laws referred to as the Black codes - laws that required Black Americans to sign yearly contracts. These were vagrancy laws meant to limit the movements of Black people, control their employment options, and maintain the idea that Blacks were inferior to Whites. In essence, a Black person could be declared vagrant, be arrested, and fined if he/she were unemployed or did not have a permanent residence. If the person could not pay the fine, that person would be forced into a labor contract to pay off the debt. The following is an example of a vagrancy law enacted by the state legislature of Mississippi in 1865:

> Section 2. Be it further enacted, that all freedmen, free Negroes, and Mulattoes in this state over the age of 18 years found on the second Monday in January 1866, or thereafter, with no lawful employment or business, or found unlawfully assembling themselves together either in the day or nighttime, and all White

persons so assembling with freedmen, free Negroes, or Mulattoes, or usually associating with freedmen, free Negroes, or Mulattoes on terms of equality, or living in adultery or fornication with a freedwoman, free Negro, or Mulatto, shall be deemed vagrants; and, on conviction thereof, shall be fined in the sum of not exceeding, in the case of a freedman, free Negro, or Mulatto, $150, and a White man, $200, and imprisoned at the discretion of the court; the free Negro not exceeding 10 days, and the White man not exceeding 6 months. Section 5. Be it further enacted, that all fines and forfeitures collected under the provisions of this act shall be paid into the county treasury for general county purposes; and in case any freedman, free Negro, or Mulatto shall fail for 5 days after the imposition of any fine or forfeiture upon him or her for violation of any of the provisions of this act to pay the same, that it shall be, and is hereby made, the duty of the sheriff of the proper county to hire out said freedman, free Negro, or Mulatto to any person who will, for the shortest period of service, pay said fine or forfeiture and all costs.

The subjugation of Blacks was necessary if White supremacy was to prevail. During Reconstruction, Blacks became the scapegoat and the reasoning behind many controversies and exploitation for the following political, social, and economic ideas: (1) The fear that "uppity" Blacks would threaten the culture and racial purity of the superior White people; (2) The efforts of lower class Whites to seize power from White merchants and landowners who controlled the vote of indebted Black tenants; (3) The desire for the elite Whites to thwart the efforts of these lower class Whites; (4) The fear of progressive White reformers that illiterate White and Black voters could be manipulated; (5) The fear of rebellious White politicians that the Black vote might prevail if southern Whites split their votes because of struggles within political parties; (6) The fear fueled by the White press which spread propaganda stories about Black crime; (7) The emergence of the pseudo-science of eugenics that led to acceptance of the views of Black inferiority; (8) The continued depiction of Blacks as lazy, stupid, and less than human in the popular minstrel shows, side shows, and circuses by Whites. (Davis, 2008)

In the years following the end of Reconstruction, the South re-established many of the provisions of the Black codes in the form of the so-called "Jim Crow laws." These remained firmly in place for almost a century, but were finally abolished with the passage of the Civil Rights Act of 1964.

After the Emancipation, southern Whites were determined to keep Blacks subordinate. Again laws were created for this purpose. These laws were a part of what is called the "Jim Crow" era; a term that originated around 1830 with a White minstrel performer named Thomas Dartmouth Rice, (Daddy Rice) who would blacken his face and dance a jig to derogate the image of Black men. There are many speculations as to who Jim Crow really was. Some said he was a Cincinnati, Ohio slave; others said he was a slave from Charleston, S.C.; others said he was a slaveholder name Crow; still others said it was a simile, Black as a crow. Regardless of the origin, Jim Crow was a demeaning and derogatory term. In the popular culture of that day, the term Jim Crow became synonymous with other stereotypical terms such as, Sambos, Coons, and Zip Dandies, all of which were meant to denigrate Blacks. After the Civil War, laws began to emerge all across the former Confederacy, called Jim Crow Laws, which legalized segregation and disenfranchisement of Blacks.

These Jim Crow Laws gained more significance when the Supreme Court ruled that the Civil Rights Act of 1875 was unconstitutional. The Act stated that "all persons...shall be entitled to full and equal enjoyment of the accommodations, advantages, facilities, and privileges of inns, public conveyances on land or water, theaters, and other places of public amusement." However, the law was rarely enforced and in subsequent civil rights cases, the Supreme Court deemed this act unconstitutional. The court's ruling was the result of complaints by Blacks involving discrimination and segregation on railroads and other public sites. The Act was challenged in 1883, and was deemed unconstitutional by the Supreme Court, on the basis that Congress had no power to regulate the conduct of individuals. The judge held that the 14th Amendment (1868), which guaranteed all citizens, ex-slaves included, equal protection under the law, only applied to states, not individuals or private companies. The court's decision was that Blacks were not denied their rights if they had separate but equal public accommodations. Of course, the majority of Blacks were not able to finance accommodations equal to Whites at that time; they had only been emancipated a short time; they were uneducated and unemployed.

Before long, Southern states passed all kinds of laws, restricting Blacks from using public areas, accommodations, and transportation. "White Only," "Colored," "Negroes and Freight" signs began to appear. These signs appeared on water fountains, restrooms, waiting rooms, entrances and exits to all public buildings, and trains. Towns began to establish curfews for Blacks, and even prohibited them from working in the same places of employment as Whites. By the 1890s, states enacted laws prohibiting Black men from voting.

Undergirding these laws was a Southern "Paramilitary" organization called the Ku Klux Klan. Their first national meeting in 1867, was organized by Confederate generals, colonels, church members, and politicians. Their tactics: fear, murder, rape, terrorism by night, political assassination, and economic intimidation, were used to control Blacks' upward mobility in society, and to maintain the status quo of White supremacy and Jim Crow.

I remember my mother and aunts, who were from Virginia, telling me of the terror they experienced as the KKK rode through their neighborhoods at night; vandalizing and beating Black people to instill fear in them. They had no recourse for this problem because these KKK members were city officials, and other people in power.

Jim Crow spread across America and engulfed the first half of the 20th century. However, it was never an acceptable condition for Blacks, and they found ways to resist and survive. They were determined to win back the civil rights that were stolen from them after the emancipation.

Some of their efforts were individual acts of defiance; some were carried out through organized resistance, such as the National Association for the Advancement of Colored People (NAACP). This resistance was met with many acts of violence on the part of Whites, such as lynching, murder, and burnings. However, the vast majority of Blacks were forced to live, as W.E.B. DuBois stated, "behind the veil." In other words, Blacks adopted an attitude of accommodation and appeasement. These tactics were used as a psychological ploy to exhibit a non-confrontational demeanor; they were survival tactics. At times survival meant shuffling and pretending to be irresponsible, and sometimes it meant turning the other cheek.

While the majority of Blacks worked hard to survive Jim Crow in the early 1900s, Black leaders such as W.E.B. DuBois and Booker T. Washington, fought to elevate Blacks on an educational and political level. Though the two men were at odds with each other over which strategies to use in resisting Jim Crow, each had a plan which, at the time, was formidable and necessary. Washington, who was born a slave, advocated accepting segregation for the time being in order to avoid the terror and violence which surrounded the Black community. He believed that educating the masses of Southern Blacks in the field of agriculture would help them to become self-sufficient, thereby creating a middle-class group of Blacks who could eventually challenge Jim Crow. With the help of White philanthropists, Washington founded many Black schools and colleges such as the Tuskegee Institute, and trained many Black vocational teachers.

On the other hand, W.E.B. Dubois, a Harvard educated Black and a New Englander, argued against Washington's plan of acceptance and appeasement. He strongly advocated resisting Jim Crow through vigilant protest, activism and higher education for Blacks. DuBois along with another activist, William Monroe Trotter, established the Niagara Movement for this purpose. This Niagara Movement was the precursor to the NAACP. The NAACP was an interracial organization which became the leading voice advocating legal resistance to segregation, disfranchisement, and lynching in America. Its unstinting legal investigations and lawsuits challenged segregation on a local level and eventually on a national level.

Both the strategies of Washington and DuBois were significant in that they emphasized the education of Black Americans. Whether the education was industrial, or on a higher level, Black Americans recognized the importance of education in those days. Education has been an integral part of the Black American struggle for equality. So why does a gap exist in the academic achievement between Black students *vis-à-vis* White students in the 21st century?

This questions leads me to the final segment of this book:

Social Stigma Legacy: The Legacy that Slavery Left for Future Generations

THE IMPACT OF SLAVERY: Its Effects On
The Academic Achievement of Black Students Today

CHAPTER 6

The Social Stigma Legacy

The answer is that nearly 300 years of chattel slavery had an unmistakable impact on the lives of Black Americans even into the 21st century. The social construct of racism was the basis for the institution of slavery, and concomitant with the struggle to survive as a slave was the struggle to be educated. Laws against educating Blacks undermined their struggle for education, but did not prevent it. Blacks have had to cope with either no formal education, or a separate system of education. Slavery set the course for separation of Blacks and Whites in education, and Jim Crow maintained that course. Of course, the disenfranchisement of Blacks in every sector of society, and particularly in education, had to take its toll.

Black males in particular appear to be suffering the most in education. Not only is there a significant gap in academic achievement scores between Caucasians and Black Americans, but The National Medical Association, (NMA) a group of some 20,000 Black American doctors, say that Black American males have been misdiagnosed with hyperactivity disorder, and as a result, are over-represented in Special Education. Black males are also over-represented in the emotionally disturbed classes.

In addition, research shows that there are stereotypes that exists about the ability of Black students to learn, which causes some teachers to treat them differently.

As a result, Black students become disengaged and distrustful so they don't perform well. If the paramount issue in a student's life is confronting a negative social identity, then it can be deduced that academic achievement will certainly be threatened.

In August 2000, Congress authorized the United States Department of Interior to do a study on the history of desegregation in public education. The study was entitled *Racial Desegregation in Public Education in the United States: National Historic Landmark Survey.* The organizations involved in the study were the National Park Service, National Conference of State Historic Preservation Officers and, Organization of American Historians. Although the study includes the struggles of other people of color, namely of Asian Americans, Native Americans, and Chicano/Latino-Americans, there is an in-depth examination of Black Americans and their quest for educational equity and empowerment in public education. This study also treated the struggles of Blacks attending higher educational institutions, however for the intended purpose of this writing, I focused on primary and secondary schools.

The study was divided into three time periods. The first period depicts the beginnings of the   Black American struggle for education in the early 1700's, up to the *Plessy vs. Ferguson* (1896) decision, which made separate but equal facilities constitutional, and resulted in segregated public schools. The second discusses the period from *Plessy vs. Ferguson,* and includes subsequent U.S. Supreme Court cases, which support segregated schools up to the first successful case against school segregation. Part three includes the case from 1954, *Brown vs. Board of Education,* in which the Supreme Court ruled that segregated schools were unconstitutional, and continues through to the 1974 Supreme Court decision in *Milliken vs. Bradley,* which placed limitations on efforts to integrate schools by busing students across city and county lines.

The committee found that despite the ban on educating Blacks during slavery, some did learn to read and write. They were either self-taught, or they were taught by sympathetic Whites. The study showed that Black Americans took advantage of every opportunity to obtain an education, and even created opportunities where none existed. No adversity or intimidation stopped their efforts to learn, because few doubted that education was, in the words of the Black American teacher, Lewis Woodson, the "jewel that will elevate, ennoble, and rescue the bodies of our long-injured race from the shackles of bondage, and their minds from the trammels of ignorance and vice."

Although this study pointed to numerous religious and philanthropic persons and organizations which helped Black American obtain an education, overshadowing their heroic efforts was the daunting effect of racism.

Here, I will cite some of the important findings of this study to give examples of the inequities of the American education system from 1700 to 1974. Moreover, this study revealed that these atrocities were prevalent throughout the North, South, East, and West. The bulleted passages are examples of the findings.

1700-1900 (Salvatore , et al, 2000)

- Of all the denominations only the Quakers initially conceived of education as a step toward the abolition of Slavery, combining physical emancipation with spiritual salvation.

- Most Southern Whites declared Blacks did not have the mental capacity to be educated, yet feared literacy would encourage escape or revolt.

- In the North, educational opportunities for Black Americans widened after the Revolution, but became increasingly segregated.

- As antagonism grew toward Black education, there were Whites and free Black Americans willing to run the risk of legal prosecution to instruct Blacks in clandestine schools.

- Most schools for Blacks in the early 19th century remained church-related – following the pattern set by Richard Allen's AME Church in Philadelphia, where the pastor doubled as the schoolmaster, teaching children during the day and their parents at night.

- In 1852 Ohio made separate schools mandatory, but even segregated schools for Blacks barely existed.

- A town meeting in New Haven in 1831, voted 700 to 3 to resist by every lawful means the establishment of a manual labor school for Blacks.

- In Canaan, New Hampshire, an angry mob of Whites employed 100 oxen to pull a Black school, the Noyes Academy, off its foundation and dump it in a swamp outside the town.

- In the North, many locales made no provision at all for the education of Black Americans and, despite being taxed to support White schools, they had to finance their own schools.

- Under-funded and overcrowded, these schools inevitably lacked the most minimal of equipment and supplies, reflecting the second-class status that Whites had forced upon Blacks. For schools for Whites, "*no expenditure is spared to make them commodious and elegant*," noted the *New York Tribune*, but those for Black Americans "*are nearly all, if not all, old buildings, generally in filthy and degraded neighborhoods, dark, damp, small, and cheerless, safe neither for the morals nor the health of those who are compelled to go to them, if they go anywhere, and calculated rather to repel than to attract them."*

- Despite almost insurmountable barriers, some 32,692 Blacks attended educational institutions on the eve of the Civil War. Against the odds, Black Americans learned; often covertly and at their peril, from slaves and free Blacks, from Whites who would teach them, and from their parents.

During the Reconstruction Era, which was from 1866 to 1876, opportunities for Blacks began to broaden and various societies to aid the freedmen were established. The climate was exciting, as these organizations sought to obtain financing to establish schools and teachers for the freedmen. The idea of freedom and education were *intertwined in the* minds of Black Americans, and they clamored for education. By 1877, over half the teachers of Black students were Black Americans, and more than 600,000 Black Americans were enrolled in school. The study also cited examples of the enthusiasm for education during this period:

- *"If I nebber does do nothing more while I live,"* proclaimed an ex-slave, "I shall give my children a *chance to go to school, for I considers education next best thing to liberty."*

- A teacher of Black soldiers stationed in Vicksburg claimed to *"have never seen such zeal on the part of pupils, nor such advancement as I see here."*

- *"Few people who were not right in the midst of the scene can form any exact idea of the intense desire which the people of my race showed for education,"* recalled Black Educator Booker T. Washington in his book, *Up from Slavery. "It was a whole race trying to go to school. Few were too young, and none too old, to make the attempt to learn. As fast as any kind of teachers could be secured, not only were day-schools filled, but night-schools as well."*

- The Black writer and scholar W. E. B. DuBois agreed, that the Black American quest for education *"was, one of the marvelous occurrences of the modern world; almost without parallel in the history of civilization."*

School integration would remain rare in the 19th century outside of New England, but even in the New England States, though laws were passed to integrate schools, de facto segregation remained a fact of life.

In the western states, the situation was no different. For example, back in 1852, when California became a state, it codified school segregation. In 1854, *The First State Convention of Colored Citizens of the State of California* met and publicly denounced this new law. *"You have been wont to multiply our vices and never to see our virtues...you receive our money to educate your children and refuse to admit our children into the common schools."*

By 1870, California established a formula of ten which meant that when Black Americans, Asian Americans, or American Indians numbered ten students, separate school districts were created for Whites and non-White children. In some cases, local school officials even offered a small fee to Black schools to enroll Mexican Americans, who were also barred from local public schools.

Southern States were against any kind of education for Black Americans. They wanted to maintain the status quo of White supremacy. They thought that educated Blacks would refuse servile jobs and field work, and that they would have to compete with Blacks for better jobs. To discourage Black education, Whites would resort to violent tactics, and even go so far as torch schoolhouses.

Former slaveholders finally wrested control of the South again through a political manipulation called the Compromise of 1877. This was a compromise regarding the election of 1876. Neither presidential candidates Rutherford B. Hayes, nor Samuel J. Tilden had enough Electoral College votes to win the presidency, therefore in a behind the scenes negotiation Hayes would be elected if he agreed to certain conditions. One of these conditions was to withdraw federal troops from the South. These troops were protecting Black Americans during the Reconstruction period, and their withdrawal essentially ended the Reconstruction Era.

Towards the end of the Reconstruction period, the enthusiasm for racial equality in the political arena began to wane, and the emergent "Jim Crow" laws, began to supplant all other legal efforts to obtain racial equality not only in education, but in every aspect of Black life. The only kind of education that would appease Whites was the kind that would keep Blacks subservient, separated, and under their control.

By the 1880s, funding for Black education was minimal at best. By 1900, though Black Americans comprised about one-third of the school-age population in the South, they only received 12% of public school funds. Some examples of funding distributions are as follows:

In 1898, Florida appropriated $5.92 per capita for White education and $2.27 for the education of Blacks; South Carolina $3.11 and $1.05 respectively. In 1900, Adams County, Mississippi, spent $22.25 for the schooling of each White student and just $2 per Black student, and the gap would continue to widen for the next third of a century.

The predominant attitude of Whites at that time was evidenced in a statement by then Governor Allen D. Chandler of Georgia who stated, "I do not believe in the higher education of the darky. He should be taught the trades, but when he is taught the fine arts, he gets educated above his caste and it makes him unhappy."

Additionally, a statement, in 1899, by A. A. Concanon, the Mississippi Superintendent of Education easily confirms this attitude, "Our public school system is designed primarily for the welfare of the White children of the state and incidentally for the Negro children." The same source revealed that Southern Black teachers were paid only one-third the salary of White teachers. Also, in order for Black students to be available during the planting and harvesting seasons, they went to school 59 days less than their White counterparts.

Eventually, industrial institutes for Black Americans like Tuskegee grew and prospered, because the prevailing belief at that time was that the only suitable learning for Blacks was to perform manual labor, to serve the needs of Whites, and not challenge White Supremacy. It was the kind of education designed to allay the fears of Whites and to adjust Blacks to a subordinate caste.

As I stated earlier, Booker T. Washington, who operated many of these industrial schools, trained Blacks to maintain a docile and accommodating attitude in order to avoid the violence and terror that surrounded the Black community. Furthermore, without this kind of training, he would not have been able to get the funding he needed for his schools. Essentially, it was the White politicians of the South and the Northern philanthropists who funded Washington's schools, and who made sure that Washington's views on educating and training Black Americans were perpetuated. Thus, at the turn of the century, when changes in industrialization and technology were burgeoning, Black Americans had to subsist on an education that was limited to training in manual and/or farm labor.

Nevertheless, Black Americans did all they could to survive and educate themselves. They attended whatever school or organization available in order to make life better. They opened businesses, and thousands migrated to the North to find work and education. *1900 – 1954 (Salvatore, et al, 2000)*

By the turn of the century, segregated schools had become sanctioned by law throughout the country. *Plessy vs. Ferguson* (1896), which ruled in favor of racially segregated schools under the premise of "separate but equal," was the foundation for what had become a way of life in America. However, in practically every instance, throughout the country, education was separate and *unequal (italics added).* Access to resources was extremely limited, as funds were geared towards the universal education of southern White children.

This shortage of resources, i.e., money, schools, Black teachers, along with overcrowded conditions, led to a decline of Blacks attending school in the first decade of the 20th century.   According to this study, nearly two-thirds of Black children between the ages of five and fourteen did not attend school.

By   1917,   however,   a   philanthropist   named   Julius Rosenwald, helped to alter the course of Black education.   He established   a   building   fund   which   provided supplementary support for building schools for Black Americans in the rural South.

The provisions for obtaining these funds mandated that the money, property, buildings, and materials be deeded to the local school officials.   In addition, people participating in this program had to raise an amount equal to or greater than   that   provided by   the   fund.   Black   Americans were   deeply   committed to   this   program,   and   their contributions to the fund exceeded all others.

By 1932, there were approximately 5,000 elementary schools built for Black American children in the rural South, and school attendance increased from 36% in 1900 to 79% by   1932.   These   little   one-room   schools   were   still insufficient   by   White   standards,   and   Black   teachers earned painfully less than their White counterparts. Still Black Americans assiduously pursued their education, and made the most of their situation.

However, the success of the Rosenwald Building Program was not entirely based on the benevolence of the

White community. The massive migration of Black Americans to the North generated enough concern so that the U.S. Department of Labor specifically encouraged support for Black schools as a means to keep the Negroes in the South and make them satisfied with their lot.

The situation in the North was not much different. Because of the rapid influx of Black Americans into northern cities, strict residential boundaries were created by the authorities to force them into racially segregated communities. In addition, dual school districts for Blacks and Whites were created by school officials who gerrymandered district lines. In some cases, segregation was also achieved by separating Black and White students into separate buildings on the same plot of land, and even separate classrooms within the same building.

At the same time, some Black Americans advocated separate districts, because of White violence against Blacks in the city, and because of the mistreatment of Black students by White teachers. Also, Black teachers generally supported the idea of separate schools, because they could not work in White schools.

Many Blacks were equally as adamant in their fight against segregated schools, citing the obvious inferiority of the Black schools and their limited opportunities for Black Americans. Thus, with the Black community divided, and resources scarce, not much could be done to stem Jim Crow and the overwhelming White sentiment to enforce segregation.

While Black Americans continued their personal quest for a good education, the NAACP waged a legal campaign to fight discrimination. In 1925, the NAACP secured a grant from the Garland Fund, named for its benefactor, Charles Garland, to investigate public financing of Black and White schools in several southern states. The investigation uncovered gross inequities in how the public funds were distributed, citing a per capita spending gap of two to one to as much as eight to one in favor of White schools.

By the 1930s, the NAACP gained enough momentum and finances to lead a continuous legal campaign for equal education. In a very significant case, *Murray vs. Pearson,* the NAACP challenged the separate but equal law and prevailed against Maryland University. The case involved a Black man, Donald Murray, who applied to Maryland University and was told that they did not admit Black people. Two brilliant Black lawyers, Charles Houston and his protégé, Thurgood Marshall, tried the case on the premise that the university had to accept Murray, because there were no separate Black law schools, and that the university was in violation of the 14th Amendment. The court ruled on behalf of Murray and in 1936, he was admitted to the law school.

Although this case did not pertain to the public schools, I cited it because it was the beginning of a long and hard fought struggle against the desegregation of public schools. The court's ruling in this case laid the foundation upon which Thurgood Marshall and others based their arguments for desegregation.

A series of similar cases regarding inequalities of budgets, salaries, and facilities led to the famous *Brown vs. Board of Education* in 1954. Marshall and his team had decided to forget fighting for equalization, but launched an all-out attack on Jim Crow itself; for desegregation and/or integration.

Brown vs. Board of Education consisted of several cases which the court placed under one heading, because the issue in each case dealt with institutionalized segregation. This case was argued in the lower courts before finally moving to the Supreme Court.

Besides arguing against the inferior conditions of Black schools, another important point that Marshall and his associates raised was the fact that the impact of segregation on White and Black children was negative. One of the sociologists, Louisa Hall testified that:

> *Segregation of White and colored children in public schools has a detrimental effect upon the colored children. The impact is greater when it is sanctioned by law; for the policy of separating the races is usually interpreted as denoting inferiority of the Negro group. A sense of inferiority affects the motivation of a child to learn.*

Segregation with the sanction of law therefore, has a tendency to retard the educational and mental development of Negro children, and to deprive them of some of the benefits they would receive in a racially integrated school system.

When the case finally reached the Supreme Court, the judge ruled in favor of Brown, recognizing that separate was most definitely in every case, never equal, and therefore violated the 14th Amendment, which guaranteed equal protection under the law. *1954-1974 (Salvatore, et al, 2000)*

The Civil Rights Act of 1964, gave further impetus to the movement toward integration. The federal government under President John F. Kennedy forbade racial discrimination in any program which received federal funds. The Law not only provided more federal oversight to the desegregation of schools, it also created a quantifiable means to assess the programs of school desegregation. The school districts had to show that there was a growth in the percentage of Black children attending their schools.

However, even with all the government oversight and the threat of withdrawal of government funding, de facto segregation remained entrenched in many districts throughout the nation.

In the case of *Milliken vs. Bradley (1974)*, for example the court decision exempted Michigan suburban districts from assisting in the desegregation of inner-city school systems. The court noted that desegregation, in the sense of dismantling a dual school system, did not require any particular racial balance in each school, grade or classroom. The court also maintained that the local districts should have control over their schools. (Salvatore, et al, 2000 pgs. 87 & 102)

The study cited many other court cases that followed *Brown vs. the Board of Education*. The struggle had been long, arduous, and in many instances perilous, and it has persisted even into the 21st century. Even 155 years after emancipation, Black Americans still bear the enduring symbol of their past degradation – the slave heritage, and our society is still stratified on the basis of race, thus our schools are stratified based on race.

According to John U. Ogbu, anthropologist and professor at the University of California, Berkeley, racial stratification is the hierarchical organization of socially defined races or groups (as distinguished from biologically defined "races" or groups), on the basis of assumed inborn differences in status honor or moral worth, symbolized in the United States by skin color.

Under this definition, we assume that there is a dominant group and subordinate groups. It is the dominant group that determines the value of skin color and the amount of status honor a racial group can have. Historically, Whites

THE IMPACT OF SLAVERY: Its Effects On
The Academic Achievement of Black Students Today

have been this dominant group and Blacks have been the subordinate group in America.

Ogbu and others have stated that the school performance gap was created by racial stratification. Racial stratification has created inferior schools, prejudice against Black students, apathy, distrust, and low performance on the part of Black students. Let's not forget that this style or type of racism is the offspring of slavery.

As a matter of fact, in 2008, then President-Elect Barack Obama, spoke about this achievement gap between Black and White students during his campaign for the presidency. The issue of race reared its ugly head, simply because he was a Black man running for president of the United States. He felt the exigency of addressing the issue of racism, and in his speech, he touched on the issue of inferior schools and the achievement gap. The following is an excerpt from his speech, "A More Perfect Union"

> *Race is an issue we can't afford to ignore. The fact is the comments that have been made and the issues that have surfaced over the last few weeks, reflect the complexities of race in this country, that we've really never worked through – a part of our union that we have not yet made perfect. Understanding this reality requires a reminder of how we arrived at this point. As William Faulkner once wrote, 'The past isn't dead and buried, in fact, it isn't even past.' We*

do need to remind ourselves that so many of the disparities that exist between the African American community and the larger American community, today can be traced directly to inequalities passed on from an earlier generation that suffered under the brutal legacy of slavery and Jim Crow. Segregated schools were and are inferior schools. We still haven't fixed them, 50 years after Brown vs. Board of Education, and the inferior education they provided, then and now, helps explain the pervasive achievement gap between today's Black and White students."

As Obama stated, and research has discovered, one of the causes for this achievement gap is related to inferior schools. As I have previously pointed out, Black Americans have always had to cope with inferior schools and strict residential boundaries that forced them to be segregated from Whites.

The better schools receive greater funding which means more services, supplies, support staff, and reduced teacher-pupil ratios which translates into higher test scores. However, traditionally, schools within the Black American areas receive substantially less funding than schools in the White areas, and 21st century schools that have a concentration of Black Americans and other minorities, still receive less funding, because in many states, local property taxes are the basis for school funding.

> *"Within most large urban school districts (those with enrollment over fifty thousand) the quality of public education offered depends on two factors: first, the socioeconomic and educational levels of the parents in the local elementary school's neighborhood; second, the academic magnet programs offered to secondary students citywide, sixth - twelfth grades."*   *(Conrad, et al 2005, p. 292)*

We are aware that although Black Americans have made great socio-economic gains, they still lag behind Whites in socio-economic status. Overcoming the tremendous obstacles presented by slavery has hindered our socio-economic status at best.

If socio-economic status is a factor in quality education, then America owes Blacks for years of deprivation and discrimination, which has kept the Black community from rising to greater economic freedom.

Who knows where Black people would be economically, if it had not been for slavery and other forms of discrimination based on the color of our skin? If we had been afforded the same opportunities as Whites in this nation, if our children had been given the same quality education as Whites, there would be no gap. A gap is a separation of some sort.

Without a separation, there is no gap; but the separation was created by racism born of slavery.

There is also the issue of magnet schools, which were originally intended to promote academic desegregation. However, in recent years, rather than increasing diversity, the focus of the magnet school has changed to selecting students based on academic achievement. These schools spend about $200.00 more on their students and offer a greater academic experience to their students than regular public schools. Although they are a part of the public school program, magnet schools do not have to adhere to school zone policies and are meant to attract students from across school zones.

Students who attend magnet schools achieve greater academic success than students who attend regular schools in the same district, and because of their student selection process, they attract the best and the brightest from all areas. A study by the Citizens Commission on Civil Rights in conjunction with Vanderbilt University revealed that students of low socioeconomic status (SES) were underrepresented in magnet schools, and that when low SES students did attend magnet schools, they fared much better academically, and were more apt to graduate high school.

Critics of Magnet schools point out that their selection process excludes students who could really benefit from their curriculum. They maintain that school districts should focus on making all schools in effect magnet schools. Here again, we see that students who could really benefit (namely Blacks) from a school that spends more money on their students, are not being selected.

Another force that has been identified as a cause of this achievement gap, is the way Blacks have been perceived and treated. Associated with this slavery legacy, is the idea of *stigma,* or spoiled social identity. That stigma is based on negative stereotypes, which have been attached to Black Americans in general. Stereotypes will be discussed later in this writing.

Stigma, however, is a construction of society, rather than an attribute of individuals. The experience of being chattel slaves stigmatized Blacks, and generated the mistreatment Blacks have received from Whites throughout the history of America. In a social setting, and particularly a school setting, stigmatization can cause a student to feel uncertain about whether or not he or she belongs in that setting.

I can attest to this, and I am sure most Blacks can. I have been in many settings where I did not feel connected to the people in that setting, and mainly because they were primarily, by majority, White. Due to what I knew about Black/White relationships in America, it was easy to feel disconnected.

Research shows and even common sense will tell you that the average person wants to feel like they belong; they want to be respected and appreciated. We know that young people in particular are sensitive; they need to know that they are loved and appreciated. In a setting where you know that the color of your skin may be an issue for someone else, it is very difficult to feel loved and appreciated.

As a former school teacher, I have heard students bully and poke fun at someone because of their race. I have seen teachers and other school personnel prefer White students over Blacks, even when Blacks were more qualified. I repeat, if the paramount issue in a student's life is confronting a negative social identity, then it can be deduced that academic achievement will certainly be threatened. Students, especially teens, want to feel connected; they need to belong. That's why gangs are so successful in recruiting teens; they give them a sense of belonging.

As mentioned in previous sections of this writing, Black Americans have been plagued with stereotypes about their ability to learn. These stereotypes, born of slavery and institutional racism, can inhibit academic performance by causing stress and worry about what people think about you.

A study by R.F. Ferguson, researcher for the Brookings institute of Washington, D.C., showed that teachers regarded the academic potential of Black and White students differently, and that this perception was based on race.   Because if this perception, teachers were not as supportive of Black students as they were of White students, and they treated Black students differently. R.F, Ferguson also asserted in 1998 that:

> *Stereotypes of Black intellectual inferiority are reinforced by past and present disparities in performance, and this probably causes teachers to underestimate the potential of Black students more than that of Whites. My bottom line conclusion is that teachers' perceptions, expectations, and behaviors probably do help to sustain, and perhaps even expand the Black-White score gap.*

An interesting study by Claude Steele, an internationally celebrated social psychologist and professor at Stanford University, showed that people with a negative social identity may perform below their abilities due to the anxiety and stress caused by fear of actually confirming the negative identity or stereotype.   Steele calls this idea "stereotype threat" Among the fears that a stereotype threat produces are:

- Will I do something that would actually confirm what they think of me?

- Does this stereotype really apply to me in certain situations?

- I don't really believe this stereotype applies to me, but I'm afraid of what others think.

- Is it because I'm Black that this is happening?

These sentiments are real; I am a witness to them, and I believe that most Blacks have experienced the same thing. Having to deal with such sentiments, having to always prove who you are, and trying to focus on curriculum, can be a heavy load to carry.

As a public school teacher, I have had plenty of experience working with Black students. There is definitely a feeling of distrust for White teachers whether it is displayed or not. You cannot approach a Black student with the attitude that he/she is inferior academically. I know many White teachers who feel this way. I have had firsthand experience in that area, and the student can perceive it. If you really believe Black students are inferior, it will surface one way or the other.

My daughter was in an over-crowded kindergarten class, and it was truly a joke. I volunteered in her classroom a few days a week, because I wanted my daughter to get a good education. The teacher was on a schedule that she had to adhere to. She had too many students to service and she could not spend the time needed to ensure their success, and I'm not sure she even cared. If I had not been in that class I know for a fact that most of those students would not have gotten any schooling that particular day. In other words, because I was there to help, many of them received a lesson.

I told this same teacher that my daughter could read because I had taught her to read at home before she went to kindergarten. I asked the teacher to test her, and perhaps she could move her to 1st grade. The teacher, who just happened to be White, refused to test her. She did not believe what I was telling her and she practically ignored me. By December of that same year, she finally agreed to test her. She gave her a workbook and my daughter finished it in a matter of days. After the Christmas holidays the teacher agreed that she should be promoted to 1st grade right away and not wait for the school year to end.

When my daughter was in the 2nd grade, her teacher recommended her for the Gifted and Talented Education program (G.A.T.E.). The person who was supposed to give her the test tried to discouraged me by saying that only White students really qualified for that program. This was around 1988. I told her to give her the test anyway. Well, she passed the test, but the area she did not do so well in had to do with puzzles. The tester tried to tell me that even though she passed the test, she probably would not do well in the class because of the section on puzzles. I called the board of education in that area and told them about this; she was subsequently fired, and my daughter went onto become one of the better students in the G.A.T.E. class, all the way up through middle school. She won many gold medals for academic competitions and performances.

As a matter of fact, she was #1 in her college class, because I instilled the value of education in all of my children and was privileged to give them the support they needed.

I was one of the privileged few, who was blessed to be home with their children in their early years of schooling. I was able to support them in their homework, and make sure they were fed properly and got a good night's sleep. On the other hand, I know many Black students who have missed so much schooling because of home circumstances, lack of money, lack of parental guidance; (mom and dad may be working two jobs trying to make ends meet), and even lack of good health care.

Missing school because of home circumstances, over-crowded classes, lack of student services and supplies, and/or minimal or no support staff, all translate into inferior education, and inferior education means low test scores. All of these circumstances are the results of the slavery legacy and the social stigma that is attached to that legacy.

How Black students respond to social stigma, is of utmost importance, because their response is the proof that something must be done to improve the quality of their education.

Research has shown that Black students believe that education and hard work is the key to success, but that hard work does not necessarily translate into success for them because of racial injustices, prejudice, and discrimination.

Therefore, they may resist the expectations of a White society.

Besides that, Black American students also have their culture to consider. It is a rich culture that is influenced by those in the student's immediate environment – people whom they know and trust, and who have had the same experiences as they have had. Therefore, they may resist the person who doesn't understand them, whose values and preferences are different from theirs. This is because school curriculum is basically Eurocentric, and it does not readily incorporate other cultures. It may include a reference to another culture, but only from a Eurocentric point of view. Shakespeare is great, but so are many other extraordinary Black poets and playwrights. There are many great Black people in History, but why are they only mentioned during Black History month? Why aren't they in the mainstream of the educational curriculum?

Black students do not see an image of who they are in the mainstream curriculum. Consequently, they have mistakenly associated academic achievement with "acting White." However, the truth is that studying, getting good grades, working hard, and being intelligent, is not based on the color of our skin. These are things that our ancestors knew were right; they knew that education was the way up. This is why Black students need to know the truth of who they are, their true culture; not the slave culture or mentality. They need to know that they come from a strong people who have overcome a multitude of degradation to get where we are today.

They need to know that it was our ancestors' belief in God, hard work, and intelligence, that has brought us this far. They need to know these things not to engender blame or guilt, but the truth must be faced in order to foster a better understanding between the two groups – Black and White.

I believe I have made it clear in this book how racism was created, and we are all victims. We must transcend this racism and live out the American creed that all men and women are created equal. We cannot sweep racism under the rug forever. It will always resurface, if we do not fix it. It's the elephant in every room where Blacks and Whites gather.

Recognizing that racism has been the root of all of the inequities in the education of Black American students, steps must be taken to overtly dismantle every inequity and right every wrong. Black American students have been cheated out of a quality education. America must redeem the time when they should have been getting a quality education. No, we cannot change the past, but we can change the future. States must allocate the funds needed to make all schools in the Black communities comparable to magnet schools. Black students are owed this. Funding schools can no longer be based on local taxes, because the poorer neighborhoods cannot afford it. I know that if the states look hard enough, they can find the money.

Teachers must recognize that the stereotype threat is ever present.   They must make proactive efforts to change their negative attitude towards Black American students' ability to learn, and treat them with respect as human beings. When a student has a good rapport with a teacher, that student is more open to receive helpful feedback, and can take advantage of other opportunities to learn.

Furthermore, educators must develop a new paradigm of curriculum which incorporates the true culture and contributions of all ethnic groups – not just a stereotyped representation of a group. This is accomplished by allowing each group to decide what represents them. Students learn best when they have a sense of belonging.

CONCLUSION

The history of the enslavement of Black Americans is undoubtedly connected to the academic achievement of Black American students. The experience of nearly 300 years of chattel slavery has taken its toll on the cultural, economic, political, and social/psychological lives of Black Americans.

Historic literature shows that the slaves themselves, placed a high value on education, and took advantage of every opportunity to learn, even to their peril. Furthermore, after slavery, and during the Reconstruction Era, when freedom was sweet and hopes were high, Black Americans clamored for an education. Several thousand freedmen obtained some form of education. However, at the end of the Reconstruction period, hopes were dashed once more, and this point in their post-slavery lives became the nadir of Black American educational experience. Since then, educational endeavors have become limited and arduous for most, because of the negative social identity or stigma passed on from slavery.

Racism has undermined the efforts of Black Americans to integrate into the mainstream of the American dream. One major aspect of the American dream is obtaining a good education. The research presented in this writing shows that inferior schools, White treatment of Black American students, and the response by Black American students to overt and covert racism, has helped to perpetuate the educational gap between Black and White students.

This phenomenon is the direct result of the stigma of slavery, the effects of which are rooted and grounded in the current educational system. Inferior schools still exist in the 21st century, and Black Americans, along with other ethnic minorities, make up much of the student body of these schools.

Opportunities for Black Americans have changed significantly, but the racial divide is immediately invoked whenever Black Americans and Caucasians interact, whether spoken or unspoken; color manages to distinguish itself first. We were all taught to think this way; it is not a natural reaction.

Furthermore, the Black American students are still plagued with the burden of "acting white" while trying to maintain a black identity. In other words, a White cultural identity is still the accepted norm if a person wants to be successful in American society.

This review of literature reveals that Black Americans in general, are an extremely strong and resilient group of people, who have made great strides and have overcome tremendous odds in the face of adversity.

There are those who would maintain the status quo; who still want to keep Black people down. I say to you, that time is over. We cannot go backwards; we must move forward and do the right thing by providing quality education to our Black students.

ABOUT THE AUTHOR

Dr. Patricia McQueen

Dr. McQueen has been an educator for over 20 years, working with at-risk and low educational achievers and exercising her expertise by providing, creating, and facilitating classes, workshops, and more for her students. Her greatest passion has been to motivate them to want to learn, teach them how to learn, and to help them move into the mainstream of American education, so they can become responsible and productive members of our society.

She earned a Master's degree in Education from California State University, Pomona, and a PhD in Biblical Studies from Next Dimension University in Rancho Cucamonga, California where she taught a college writing class.

Dr. McQueen is a mother, grandmother, educator, and entrepreneur. Some may know Dr. McQueen as a recording artist, with several Gospel CD's.

However, education has always been in the forefront of her life, and she believes that this book will help bring dramatic changes in American education. This in effect, will help bring our Black American students into the mainstream, *and* remove the stigma that the Institution of Slavery has passed down from generation to generation.

THE IMPACT OF SLAVERY: Its Effects On
The Academic Achievement of Black Students Today

REFERENCES

Allen, T. (2002). The *invention of the white race: Racial oppression and social control.* New York: Verso.

American Anti-Slavery Group. (2007)

Retrieved from:

http.iabolish.com/modernslavery. [101].

Bennett, L., Jr. (1975). The Shaping of Black America. Chicago: Johnson Publishing

Berlak, H. (2008). Race and the achievement gap. Rethinking Schools, 15 (4).

Retrieved from:

http://www.rethinkingschools.org/archive/15 04/Race15 4.shtml.

Blassingame, J. (1977) Slave testimony: Two centuries of letters, speeches, interviews, and autobiographies. Baton Rouge: Louisiana State University Press.

Blassingame, J., Hinks, P., & McKivigan, J. (Eds). (2003). The Frederick Douglass papers. New Haven: Yale University Press.

Brown v. Board of Education: About the case. (2008). Retrieved from:

http://brownvboard.org/summary

Chen, G. (2003). What is a magnet school? Public School Review.

Retrieved from:

http://www.publicschoolreview.com/articles/2

Clinton, C. (2004), Harriet Tubman: The Road to Freedom.
New York: Little Brown Book Company

CNN.com. (2007). Extra! History of Black History Month.
Retrieved from:
http://cnnfyi.printthis.clickability.com/pt/cpt?action=cp
t&title=History +of+ Black+ History

Cohen, G. & Garcia, J. (2008). Identity, belonging, and
achievement: A model, interventions, implications.

Current Directions in Psychological Science.
Retrieved from:
http://www3.interscience.wiley.com/journal/121561294
abstract?CRETRY=1&SRETRY=0

Conrad, C., Whitehead, J., Mason, P., & Stewart, J. (Eds.).
(2005). African Americans in the U.S. Economy.
Lanham, Md.: Rowman & Littlefield, Inc.

Crocker, J. & Major, B. (1989). Social Stigma and Self-
Esteem: The Self-Protective Properties of Stigma.
Psychological Review, 96, 608-630.
Retrieved May 10, 2007 from:
http://ovnweb.hwwilsonweb.com.opac.librarycsupomon
a.eu/hww/results/resultssingle

Croizet, J. Despres, G. Gauzins, M. Huguet, P. Leyens, J. &
Meot, A. (2004).
Stereotype Threat Undermines Intellectual Performance
by Triggering Disruptive Mental Load.

Retrieved from:

http://sagepub.com/cgi/content/abstsract/30/6/721

Davis, C. & Gates, H. (Eds.). (1985). The Slave's Narrative. Oxford: University Press.

Davis, R. (2008, July 2). Creating Jim Crow: In-Depth Essay. Retrieved from:

http://www.jimcrowhistory.org/history/creating2.htm

De Tocqueville, A. and Beaumont, G. (1999). Marie, or Slavery in the United States: A Novel of Jacksonian America. Baltimore: Johns Hopkins University Press.

Dorsey, A. (2007). Black History is American History: Teaching African American History in the 21st century. The Journal of American History, 93(4). Retrieved May 23, 2007, from:

http://0www.historycooperative.org.opac.library.csupo mona.edu/journals/jah/93.4/Dorsey

Ferguson, R. (1998). Teachers' Perceptions and Expectations and the Black-White Test Score Gap. Urban Education, Vol. 38, No. 4, 460-507 Retrieved from:

http://uex.sagepub.com/cgi/content/abstract/38/4/460

Finkelman, Paul (Ed.). (1977). Slavery and the Law. Madison: Madison House.

Ford, D. Grantham, T. & Whiting, G. (2008). Another Look at the Achievement Gap: Learning from the Experiences of Gifted Black Students. Urban Education, 43(2).

Retrieved from:

http://uex.sagepub.com.

Furrer, C. & Skinner, E. (2003). Sense of Relatedness as a Factor in Children's Academic Engagement and Performance. Journal of Educational Psychology, 95(1), 148-162.

Goffman, E. (1963). Stigma: Notes on the Management of Spoiled Identity. Upper Saddle River, N. J.: Prentice Hall.

Goldstone, L. (2005), Dark Bargain. Slavery, Profits, and the Struggle for the Constitution. New York: Walker Publishing Co.

Goodell, W. (1968). The American Slave Codes in Theory and Practice: Its Distinctive Features Shown by its Statutes, Judicial Decisions and Illustrative Facts. New York: Johnson Reprint Corporation.

Gordon, Sharon. (2007). A Profile in History: Carter G. Woodson. The Weekly Gleaner, p. 13.

Grossman, R. Kim, S. Tan, S. & Ford, T. (2008). Stereotype Threat and Recommendations for Overcoming it: A Teaching Case Study. Retrieved March 3, 2009, from: http://www.sciencecases.org/stereotype_threat/notes.asp.

Harvey, R. (2001). Individual Differences in the Phenomenological Impact of Social Stigma. The Journal of Social Psychology, 141(2), 174-189.

Heatherton, T., Kleck, R., Hebl, M., & Hull, J. (Eds.). (2003). The social psychology of Stigma. New York: Academic Press.

Higginbotham, A., Jr. (1978). In the Matter of Color: Race and the American Legal Process: The Colonial Period. New York: Oxford University Press.

Jordan, W. J., & Cooper, R. (2003). High School Reform and Black Male Students: Limits and Possibilities of Policy and Practice. Urban Education, 38(2), 196-217.

Kunjufu, J. & Prescott, F. (1992). Self-Esteem Through Culture Leads to Academic Excellence. Chicago: African American Images.

Leary, J. (2005). Post Traumatic Slave Syndrome: America's Legacy of Enduring Injury and Healing. Milwaukie, Oregon: Uptone Press.

Loury, G. (2002). The Anatomy of Racial Inequality. Cambridge: Harvard University Press.

Lynch, Willie. (1999). The Willie Lynch Letter; & The Making of a Slave. Chicago, IL: Lushena Books.

McMillian, M. Monique. (2004). Is No Child Left Behind 'Wise Schooling' for African American Male Students? The High School Journal, 87, (2). Retrieved from: http://muse.jhu.edu/login?uri=/journals/high_school_journal/v087/87.2mcmillian.pdf

Meltzer, M. (1995). Frederick Douglass in His Own Words. Orlando: Harcourt Brace

Lookup.asp?w=trendgap2007&g=12&s=MAT&j=NT&y=200

8&v=SDRACE&vs. National Assessment of Educational Progress.

Retrieved from:

http://nationsreportcard.gov/writing_2007/w0037.asp

National Education Association. (2003-2006). The Nation's Report Card. Retrieved April 10, 2007, from: http://www.nea.org

Nation's Report Card. (2005).

http://nationsrportcard.gov/nde/reportcard/gLookup asp?w=trendgap2007&g=12&s=MAT&j=NT&y=2008 &vSDRACE&vs.

Nelson, M. (1988). Merl R. Eppse and Studies of Blacks in American History Textbooks.

Retrieved from:

http://0newfirstsearch.oclc.org.opac.librarycsupomon a.edu/WebZ/FSQUERY?format=BI

Obama, B (2008). A More Perfect Union. Retrieved from: http://cnn.com

Ogbu, J. (1994). Racial Stratification and Education in the United States: Why Inequality Persists. Teachers College Record, 96(2), 264-298.

Retrieved from:

http://eric.ed.gov/ERICWebPortal/custom/portlets/re
cordDetails/detailmini.jsp?_nfpb=true.

Orfield, G. (2008). Civil Rights Project Releases Report on Magnet Schools.

Retrieved from:

http://www.magnet.edu/modules/news/article.php?sto
ryid=47

Osborne, A. (1976). A Note on Black Economic Well-Being in the North and West.

The Review of Black Political Economy, (7)1, 85-92.

Roach, R. (2002). Black Innovation: Learning From the Past: African Americans in Technology. Black Issues in Higher Education.

Retrieved from:

http://findarticles.com/p/articles/mi_m0DXK/is_1_19
/ai_84429940/print

Salvatore, S. Martin, W. Ruiz, V. Sullivan, P. Sitkoff, H. (2000, August).

Racial Desegregation in Public Education in the United States.

Retrieved from:

http://www.nps.gov/nhl/themes/themes.htm

Schmader, T., & Johns, M. (2003). Converging Evidence that Stereotype Threat Reduces Working Capacity. Journal of Personality and Social Psychology

Retrieved from:

http://scholar.google.com/scholar?hl=en&q=author:%2
2Schmader%22+intitle:%22Converging+e

Starobin, R. (Ed.). (1974). Letters of American Slaves. New York: New Viewpoints.

Steele, C. ((1992). Race and the Schooling of Black Americans. The Atlantic Monthly, 269(4), pp.67-78.

Steele, C. & Aronson, J. (1995). Stereotype Threat and the Intellectual Test Performance of African Americans. Journal of Personality and Social Psychology, 69, 797-811.

Steele, C. M., Spencer, S. J., & Aronson, J. (2002). Contending with Group Image

The Psychology of Stereotype and Social Identity Threat. In M.P. Zanna (Ed.). Advances Experimental Social Psychology (Vol. 34, pp. 379-440). San Diego, CA: Academic Press. Retrieved from:

http://www-psych.stanford.edu/~steele/vita.html

Wachtel, Paul L. (2003). The Roots of Racism: A Psychoanalytic Perspective. Black Renaissance, 5, 45.

Walker, S. ((2001). Acknowledging our Knowledge(s) and Telling Our Stories in and on Our Own Terms. African Roots: American Culture. Lanham Md.: Rowman & Littlefield.

Walton, G. & Cohen, G. (2007). A Question of Belonging: Race, Social Fit, and Achievement. Journal of Personality and Social Psychology, 92(1), 82-96.

Woodson, C. (Ed.). (1969). The Mind of the Negro as Reflected in Letters Written During the Crisis: 1800-1860. New York: Russell & Russell.